David M____

1 of 50

A Year in the Life of
Mount Stewart

For Pat

Published by Cottage Publications,
an imprint of Laurel Cottage Ltd.
Donaghadee, N. Ireland 2012.
Copyrights Reserved.
© Text and photographs David Kirk 2012.
All rights reserved.
No part of this book may be reproduced
or stored on any media without the express
written permission of the publishers.
Design & origination in Northern Ireland.
Printed & bound in China.

ISBN 978 1 900935 92 0

Contents

Foreword   7

Introduction   9

The Setting of Mount Stewart   23

Winter – Hard Work and Magic Moments   29

Among the Trees of Mount Stewart   45

Spring into Action!   61

Lakeside Beauty   83

Summer in Full Colour   95

Gardens to Delight   111

Autumn – The Grand Finale   137

The Story of a Great Garden   161

Foreword

I take great pleasure in introducing David Kirk's wonderful pictoral record of Mount Stewart, the Northern Ireland home of my maternal grandparents where my sister, Elizabeth, and I were brought up.

It was our grandmother who created the fabulous garden and, with our mother and father, made them over to the National Trust in 1955. She continued to supervise, donate new plants and work in the garden right up to the time of her death in 1959 at the age of 80.

Less than twenty years later our mother gave the house and many of its contents to the National Trust and now I, on behalf of our family, am arranging for most of the remaining contents as well as the Mount Stewart Estate to join the holdings of the National Trust in order to preserve it all for future generations to enjoy as my sister and I did growing up here.

David Kirk's album of exceptionally beautiful photographs of the house and especially of the garden in all seasons is a wonderful tribute to my grandmother's extraordinary creativity and vision both in the garden and in the decoration of the house, but he has also faithfully recorded Mount Stewart as it is today, enjoyed by hundreds of thousands of National Trust visitors and members and cared for by their highly qualified professional staff and countless volunteers.

It is these visitors and volunteers that now bring new life to the property. Thanks to the generous hospitality of the National Trust, our family remains in residence to provide a living continuity with past generations who, over two hundred and fifty years, created a remarkable property and bequeathed it to the enjoyment of all.

Lady Rose Lauritzen
Mount Stewart 2012

I believe in God, only I spell it Nature

Frank Lloyd Wright

Introduction

When the bold Alexander Stewart, gentleman, of Donegal, decided more than 250 years ago to invest a large part of the substantial dowry that came with his new wife Mary in a swathe of promising real estate around the northern reaches of Strangford Lough he would hardly have imagined that one day a small loughside corner of it would be drawing more than 150,000 people a year to explore and delight in what it had become.

Or that the cabin he built on its rising ground as a weekend retreat, with fine views stretching from the Mourne Mountains to his other newly acquired lands around Scrabo Hill, would have become a grand mansion surrounded by one of the most beautiful gardens in Ireland – acclaimed as among the greatest in Europe.

It came to be called Mount Stewart.

Today it is an entrancing demesne of lake and lawn, exotic and mighty trees, rare flowering shrubs from every continent, secret places and, like a patchwork skirt spreading from the house, an array of formal gardens – outdoor rooms really – some whimsical, some dramatic but all colourful and elegant and ever-

A small child sculpted in bronze impishly greets those who step into the secret garden that bears her name. The child coyly posing on her fountain surrounded by beds of blue and white flowers is Mairi, born in 1921, youngest daughter of Edith, Lady Londonderry, who grew up as her mother created the Mount Stewart gardens and lived her life there, dying in 2009

changing with the seasons.

Tectonic and climatic forces shaped the landscape but a gentle human touch turned it into a garden where art and imagination, crafts and skills, nature, history (and of course great wealth) – but above all a love of growing things – have come together in an inspired symphony.

The luxuriously elegant Drawing Room of Mount Stewart - the grandest of the rooms scheduled to undergo complete redecoration (eighty years since its last) over the next few years in the National Trust's £6 million refurbishment programme of the house which will also see many more of its rooms being opened to the public.

Brightly planted classical urns herald a vista of stylish gardening

The inspiration was that of one woman – Edith, Lady Londonderry, the wife of Alexander Stewart's descendent, the Seventh Marquess, and probably the brightest socialite of her time, who in the 1920s and 30s took a fairly mundane demesne and transformed it into a uniquely outstanding part of our heritage.

Fortunately she was inspired in a further way. In her later years, being aware of the sad fate that had befallen many other wonderful 19th and early 20th century gardens following the demise of their owners or just hard times, she took a step that has ensured hers would continue to be enjoyed by future generations. The result was that for more than 60 years now her gardens have flourished under the stewardship of National Trust.

With the House itself, along with much of its furniture, sculptures and other contents – again of rich heritage value – being passed to the Trust in 1977, the package of outdoor and indoor treasures that is Mount Stewart was completed and with good reason is now revered as one of the jewels in its crown.

Few gardens, if any, can offer such a range of horticultural diversity, from groomed formal lawns and terraces to wild woodland – from Alice in Wonderland to Tolkien. People who visit Mount Stewart regularly see that it is always in a state of change: new plantings, changing colour swathes appear in the formal gardens, overgrown areas will have been cleared and planted with new saplings, new blooms appear among the hundreds of rhododendrons that are the high spot of the spring colour display, a giant beech is suddenly not there any more, wild flowers sparkle briefly in the woods where a clearance has let in the light . . .

It is an ever-evolving garden and the changes being made to it are not being made just for the sake of change. During the war and the years of austerity that followed, the gardens had inevitably deteriorated and by the time National Trust acquired them they had fallen far below the standards that had made them famous. In the first years of Trust ownership, maintenance rather than restoration was the priority but this situation has been reversed since the early 1970s and the changes being made now are part of a major six year programme to revitalise, rejuvenate and restore the garden to what had been the ideals of their creator.

The programmes involves the enhancement of unique garden features, the replacement of ones that have been lost, restoration of original planting schemes and replacement of botanically important plants that have not survived as well a continuation of the adventurous spirit in the acquisition of new plants that it is hoped will flourish in the garden' unique micro-climate.

The Trust's ambition is no less than to restore Mount Stewart's reputation as an international botanical and horticultural giant. So it is just going to keep getting better as a place to visit!

But wisely the Trust realises that to recreate a garden and have it 'frozen' in time is not realistic or desirable

Flags of every region of the British Isles fly to welcome the thousands of visitors who flock to the major events staged every year at Mount Stewart.

and its strategy is a compromise between restoring the gardens to an authentic flavour of what they were when they were created and planting schemes compatible with the pressures on the gardens of today's high visitor numbers.

'To lock the garden into a single restoration period of time would suffocate it,' its Conservation Strategy Plan states. 'The garden was and should always be a dynamic living entity, a melting pot that requires constant grooming, experimentation, nurturing and reshaping'.

And above all Mount Stewart will be maintained as a family garden, a place for relaxation and entertainment. A place to explore and enjoy.

The Trust's restoration plans are not confined to the

Exuberant cascades of wisteria froth over the balustrades of the long veranda overlooking the Italian garden

gardens. A major refurbishment costing some £6 million is under way that will not only see the renovation of the six stately rooms in the mansion at present open to guided tours but many more will also be opened up to visitors.

A Year in the Life of Mount Stewart is not a guide-book or a catalogue of its attractions – it is a leisurely ramble around it in images and words over the course of a year and the changing of the seasons, hopefully allowing its charms to be seen through new eyes and new things to be discovered by those who seek them out.

It is also a tribute to the skills and commitment of the people – staff and volunteers – whose work ensures it will continue to be there to be enjoyed.

There is a serene and settled majesty to woodland scenery that enters into the soul and delights and elevates it, and fills it with noble inclinations

Washington Irving

A duck forsakes the lake for a stroll through the formal gardens

13

Nature always wears the colours of the spirit

Ralph Waldo Emerson

Lilies and primula bring a riot of
colour to the lakeside in spring

Among the most majestic of Mount Stewart's rhododendron displays are those along the driveway between the House and 'Newtownards Lodge', the original main entrance to the estate, some of which have been welcoming visitors for well over a century.

**If the simple things of nature have a message
you understand, rejoice, for your soul is alive**

Eleanora Duse

Burnished gold by a dawn sun the Griffin keeps
an imperial eye over the 'zoo' of whimsical
animal sculptures that turn the formal Italian
Garden into a fantasy experience.

Early morning light shafts
through the trees to light the
autumn woodland floor

Proud and watchful, Mount Stewart's iconic White Stag stands on the sweeping lawn known as the Jubilee Glade waiting, as tradition has it, in readiness for the next human soul he will be called on to carry to the mythical Celtic land of eternal youth, Tir na nOg – which is the name of the nearby Londonderry family burying ground which Edith, Lady Londonderry had built on high ground overlooking the estate

One of the estate's pheasants takes a morning stroll

Built in the 1780s the Temple of the Winds, with its magnificent views of Strangford Lough from the Mountains of Mourne to Scrabo Hill, was a fine example of the 'recreational' retreats fashionable in wealthy estates of the time. This 'temple built for mirth and jollity' with its exquisitely inlaid floors, is now a popular venue for (hopefully!) more restrained functions such as wedding receptions and family celebrations. It is open for visitors to see its elegant interior on Sunday afternoons.

Appropriately ghostly, floodlit trees reflected
in the lake waters are a dramatic backdrop
to each year's Hallowe'en experience.

Autumn sets the woodlands ablaze

The turret of Tir na nOg, the Land of Eternal Youth, peeps over the autumn-changing shrubs.

The recently enlarged shop adjacent to the reception area makes for an enjoyable browsing opportunity!

The thousands of visitors who 'take the tour' of Mount Stewart House between March and October every year are led, entertained and well informed by the team of knowledgeable volunteer guides who regale them with the story of the house, its history and treasures.

One of its most valued treasures is the famous painting of champion racehorse Hambletonian by George Stubbs.

Its drumlin-top position gives the Temple of the Winds magnificent views
of Strangford country with Scrabo Tower in the distance

The Setting
of Mount Stewart

Mount Stewart gardens do have one really huge fault!

No, not something to be complained about – a geological fault, a crack in the earth's crust which runs down the Ards Peninsula, right through the gardens, the result of a massive convulsion in the earth's crust 350 million years ago. The rock west of the rupture sank, that on the east rose, creating a great valley which it is estimated could have been as much as a kilometre deep.

Over millions of years the high rock was worn down, the valley filled with successive layers of limestones and sandstones until the land was almost level again. But the remnants of the valley are still there – filled with the waters of Strangford Lough.

Walk from Mount Stewart house to behind the lake and you traverse almost 200 million years of earth history. Underlying most of the gardens are the same Triassic sandstones that form Scrabo Hill and much of the Lough shore, but a few yards from the north edge of the lake the face of a steep outcrop of hard grey Silurian rock – a remnant of the high ground – reveals the ancient fault-line.

The sun sets behind Strangford Lough, with the Mountains of Mourne lining the far horizon.

But this rock-face has another, much more recent, story to tell. Some 8,000 years ago storm-waves were breaking against it – it formed a buttress behind the cobbles and sands of the shore of a lough whose waters were up to eight metres higher than today's.

Following the melting of the ice-sheets that had covered the north of Ireland and under which the drumlin hills that rise on either side of Mount Stewart's lawns were moulded, sea levels rose dramatically creating

Waves once broke against this rocky outcrop behind the lake – marking Strangford Lough's boundary about 8,000 years ago when sea levels were up to eight metres higher than today and a wide cobble beach was formed below it. Today's lake was excavated in the 1840s by on the site of a gravel pit from which the stones were extracted for road and path making

shorelines far above the present ones. Later, relieved of their burden of ice, the land itself began to rise slowly and the shore retreated, leaving truncated drumlins with bays of raised beach between them, in one of which are Mount Stewart's gardens.

The estate's soils, derived from the thick glacial till that covers the bedrock, are not especially rich and the bay in which the gardens nestle opens to the south-west is ideally placed to funnel in the prevailing winds blasting across the Lough! Although the upper Ards Peninsula has a generally fairly mild and dry climate (by Northern Ireland standards) and a longer than average growing season it should not be an ideal situation for a luxuriant garden – certainly not for the range of rare and tender exotic plants it boasts.

Mount Stewart's gardens are there to be enjoyed because of one thing – the protecting ring of tall trees planted up to 200 years ago, and dense lower shrubs growing between them, which gives them a moist warm sheltered environment to snuggle down in.

The effectiveness of the protection the shelter belts give – especially that from the woodland area between the road and the shore – can be experienced easily. Visitors getting out of their cars on a stormy day feel the full blast of the wind blowing across the lough – but move into the garden and it is a totally different world, quiet and calm everywhere. It can be quite a shock at the end of your visit when you return to the car park!

The miles of wind and salt-burned hedges and even high trees every spring along the road on either side of Mount Stewart also show how effective and essential the shelter is for the garden. The trees planted on the high ground on the three inland sides of the estate protect it from cold northerly winds. (The pictures of the lake, frozen over for weeks in December 2010, show however that even it is not always immune to extremes of weather!)

It was her realisation of the opportunities that Mount Stewart's unique micro-climate opened up for her gardening dreams that spurred Edith, Lady Londonderry, to indulge her passion for the flamboyant and exotic.

An aerial view of the Mount Stewart gardens

Stones from the post-glacial cobble beach that underlies much of Mount Stewart's gardens – and in places make spadework more than a little difficult!

The sheltering trees made Mount Stewart what it is but they themselves are ageing; gaps are appearing and, allied to the possible threats associated with climate change such as rising sea levels, storm surges and changes in wind patterns, the National Trust is actively studying what measures need to be taken to meet such challenges for the future.

Ripple marks on stones in the garden walls tell a 230 million year old story of deserts and floods in which the local Triassic sandstone used to build the walls was formed

Mount Stewart's gardens and woods were a small part, about 90 acres, of the whole Londonderry estate – the rest is rich farmland which gives it a pleasant rural setting

A hushed stillness comes over the lakeside shrubberies as snow blankets the grass and coats branch and leaf

Green thoughts emerge from some deep source of stillness which the very fact of winter has released

Mirabel Osler

Winter
Hard Work and Magic Moments

The gates to the formal gardens are closed, but inside the clippers and mowers of summer care have given way to spade and blade as beds are cleared and turned and fed in preparation for another year's feast of colour, old shrubs are replaced or pruned, necessary repairs are made to stone and timber and planned changes to the planting schemes are prepared for.

The mansion doors are closed too but inside is not empty silence – the voices of the house guides are now replaced with the sounds of the deep cleaning and grooming that the rooms and every object and item of furniture in them are given every year – months of work before the dust sheets are whisked off in spring and the rooms opened again to visitors.

Winter may be the 'closed' season for the formal gardens and the house but for the teams who look after them it is as busy as any other behind the scenes. In the informal garden and woodland areas it is business as usual and open to visitors but here too winter is 'heavy lifting' time of year when most of jobs such as tree felling and thinning, rhododendron clearing and repairing storm damage is carried out.

It is also where winter creates some of Mount Stewart's most magic moments – your feet crunching on layers of frozen leaves as bright low sun strikes through the bare trees turning the ground to gold, bewildered birds standing on the frozen lake, the first snowdrops . . .

And if heavy snow is forecast, don't miss it – get down there fast, it won't last long!

Who says there's no colour in winter?

It is rare for the lake to freeze right across
and then a good snowfall transforms it

The snow blankets the Sunk Garden in still silence. The formal gardens are not open to visitors in the winter – the time of renovation and renewal of the beds and shrubberies

A time of slim pickins'!

Low evening sun can set the woods afire

Every gardener knows that under the cloak of winter lies a miracle – a seed waiting to sprout, a bulb opening to the light, a bud straining to unfurl. And the anticipation nurtures our dream

Barbara Winkler

Winter's farewell kiss – the flowering of the lovely
snowdrops (a number of rare exotic varieties
of which can be found in the Lily Wood)

Cyclemen splash colour on the late winter grass

From December to March there three gardens, the garden outdoors, the garden of pots and bowls in the house – and the garden of the mind's eye

Katherine S White

Low winter sun strikes through the leaves and petals of an early blooming rhododendron

Torrential downpours that are a feature of our changing weather patterns have been proving too much for the natural drainage of the gardens – here giving the Lily Wood a definite mangrove swamp look. Work is now being carried out to improve the drainage system

One of the major jobs gardeners and volunteers have to tackle now during the winter months is the clearance of the acres of Rhododendron ponticum that over a century had advanced remorselessly through the woodland areas not only destroying natural biodiversity with its dense shade and drippings of poisonous sap but now also known to be a major vehicle for the spread of deadly Sudden Oak Death fungus Phytopthera ramorum. The tangled bushes are cut by hand and chain saw and then burned in bonfires – a nice job for a cold winter day! It will be a long job but as each area is cleared it is planted with young trees to bring on a new generation of woodland.

Tomorrow's trees now flourish in areas cleared of rhododendron

The best time to plant a tree was 20 years ago. The next best time is now

Chinese proverb

Some enthusiastic rhododendrons
just refuse to wait for spring!

**In a way Winter is the real Spring – the
time when the inner things happen**

Edna O'Brien

A flock of seagulls come inland for a bit of rest and shelter – only to find it's standing only on the frozen lake

When the winter lake starts going short of food supplies, the ducks come ashore to forage for worms and other goodies on the rain-soaked lawns

Clouds of steam rise from the great compost heaps
as they are 'mined' by tractor before their rich
goodness is spread around the shrubberies. The
'cooking' of plant material in the heap produces
very high temperatures, high enough to turn
the rain that soaks through them to steam.

As overgrown areas are thinned out the plant
material is put through the chipper for composting

Waste? Rubbish!

In the course of a year of pruning and weeding, thinning overcrowded plantings, shaping shrubs and the sad but sometimes necessary felling of giant trees that have become unsafe at the end of their long lives, the caring for and managing of Mount Stewart's acres of gardens produce tons of 'waste' plant material.

But little is allowed to go to waste in a well-run estate.

Some plants such as the invasive *Rhododendron ponticum* which can be a carrier for the potentially deadly 'Sudden oak death' disease, can only be effectively disposed of by burning but virtually all of the living material cut down today will in time be returned to feed the flowers and trees and shrubs for visitors of the future to enjoy.

During the winter months the chatter of the wood-chomping 'chipper' is a regular sound in the woodlands and shrubberies as pruned branches and stems are reduced to shredded particles. These are taken to the composting facility where they are piled into huge mounds and by the end of the season there might be 200 cubic metres of material being decomposed by micro-organisms. Turned over regularly during the next year to ensure it is all broken down evenly it is then taken back and spread over the shrubberies and beds as a the richest possible feed the living plants can have.

Stems and branches too thick to go through the chipper also prove valuable in one way or another. 'Ringed', or cut to short lengths, and sold as firewood provide a valuable income source for the estate. In the woodlands they are often used to create 'eco-piles' – stacked neatly to slowly rot back over decades into the earth from which they grew, creating over time islands of habitat for micro-organisms, the insects and invertebrates that feed on them, the small animals and birds that in turn feed on *them,* and so on.

Other habitats for micro-life are created by the modern woodland management practice of leaving standing the bottom 12 or 15 feet of the trunks of big mature trees whose time has come. The ecosystem created in such a trunk as it rots is markedly different from that of a dead tree lying on the ground, creating a new diversity of life. Such 'eco-pillars' can be seen throughout Mount Stewart.

Sound trunks of mature trees can be sold to timber merchants but a much better use is found for many of them by cutting them into six feet lengths, slicing one side off to make a flat surface and placing them at strategic points around the estate as seats where visitors can take their rest and contemplate the beauty around them.

Reflections of a woodland seat

Come – rest on me. Reflect
in stillness and enjoy this place

Once high, I brushed the sky;
painted it with spring's pale green
Harvested summer suns, danced in the wind
whispered the gossip of the woods
sometimes roared in Strangford's storms.

I saw your many generations
come and grow and go.

My long life done
In six-foot lengths I lie now felled
cut and sawn flat-topped
Smoothed by the sitting
of those I long looked down on

No surge more of sap in spring
No leafy branch for bird to sing.

Now others come to me for rest
They who love to walk my woods
Contemplate their beauties
And maybe even, sometimes
think on what I once was.

Sit on me and you sit
on history.

David Kirk

A tree has to be felled – but not wasted. Soon it will be placed at a strategic site to provide a place for visitors to take a rest

Endless forms most beautiful

Charles Darwin

Among the Trees
of Mount Stewart

The tall trees that cradle Mount Stewart's gardens were originally planted for a purely practical reason – as a shelter belt, to give protection from cold north winds and south-westerly gales blasting the parkland of the developing 19th century estate from across the Lough.

Given extra height by being planted over the drumlins that surround the gardens – Clark's Hill on the east, Rose Hill on the north and McComb's Hill to the west, as well as the on the hill which gives the Temple of the Winds its panoramic views, the trees were – and still are – critical to the survival of the gardens and their unique flora.

But their practical importance is now matched by their value as a visitor attraction. For those who love to walk with nature the woodland world they have created is one of Mount Stewart's most enjoyable assets. They have taken their place along with the formal gardens, the Lily Wood and the Lakeside as a delightful element of the Mount Stewart experience in their own right.

And you don't have to enjoy the trees from the paths. With the opening up of the woods over recent years

Leave the paths and look for the hidden charms!

by the clearance of the *rhododendron ponticum* that for decades had made most of them impenetrable, it is possible to wander through virtually their whole area. Let's hope work will be done to extend the network of paths through parts of the woodland not at present open to visitors to make it even better.

In the meantime, wander off the tracks – explore!

The endless cycle – younger trees in the flush of a
new spring life stand around a venerable fallen giant

**In every walk with nature one
receives far more that he seeks**

John Muir

A small clump of conifers near the lake provides
a contrast to the broadleaved woodlands

Nature's fairy lights – a shaft of sunlight
fluoresces two rhododendron leaves that
have taken early autumn colouring

Creating eco-piles in the woodlands is a favoured way of 'recycling' small branches cut during thinning operations. Fungi and bacteria cause the wood to decay, creating a habitat for small insects and beetles, which in turn feed small mammals and birds, and all the time returning their minerals to the earth.

A fallen tree can be given a whole new life!

A benign climate and exotic plantings
give some parts of the woodlands
a distinctly tropical air

Sunlight strikes down between the trunks of high Douglas fir to illuminate a grassy glade

**Look deep into nature and then you
will understand everything better**

Albert Einstein

If there was to be a 'sacred grove' among Mount Stewart's trees this peaceful clearing on Rhododendron Hill would have to be the leading contender.

**The groves were
God's first temples**

William Cullen Bryant

Alone with myself
The trees bend to caress me
The shade hugs my heart

Candy Polgar

If a tree dies – plant
another in its place

Linnaeus

This ancient cork oak tree overhangs the Ladies Walk path between the House and the Lake

Venerable and fallen trees welcome new young ones growing around their feet

Young, old and fallen – all stages of woodland life are to be found together

Among the spring flowers lie the crumbling remains of Mount Stewart's 19th century ice house, a 'must-have' facility for any respectable estate of the time, huge below-ground chambers where game would be packed in ice and snow and kept fresh through until late spring.

Opportunistic ferns make themselves at home on a long felled tree trunk

Along the woodland track edges, where the sun gets through, conditions are perfect for glorious shows of wild flowers

Foxgloves cuddle up to a
sequoia in the Lily Wood

**Because they are primeval, because they
outlive us, because they are fixed, trees
seem to emanate a sense of permanence.
And although rooted in earth, they seem
to touch the sky. For these reasons it is
natural to feel we might learn wisdom
from them . . . some secret vital to our
real, our lasting and spiritual existence**

Kim Taplin

Still wearing their autumn garb the
beeches reach for the skies

Nature has transformed a long-fallen giant
into a piece of woodland sculpture

**I never saw a discontented tree. They
grip the ground as though they like it**

John Muir

When ancient trees become too unsafe to be allowed to continue standing, they have to be felled, the remaining sound wood put to a variety of uses, the decayed being left to crumble back into the earth

Dramatic colours contrast by the side of the main drive

Spring
into Action!

Whether Mount Stewart was made for spring or spring was made for Mount Stewart is hard to know – but they certainly get some act together!

The long winter sleep over, the gardens and woodlands wake up into an extravaganza of bright new foliage and joyful colour. Some of the magnificent rhododendrons in fact don't seem to like a long lie-in and burst into bloom in early February and over the next three months waves of reds, pinks, purples and yellows wash across the slopes, blooms reaching from ground level to the tops of towering century-old bushes.

In the formal gardens tulips and other spring bulbs splash their colour on the ground and, between the trees, the lawns at the front of the House dance yellow with meandering drifts of thousands of daffodils.

Less showy but just as moving as the exuberant show of colour the flowering plants put on is the light green brightness spreading through the woods as the trees, from the majestic beeches and venerable oaks to the hundreds of newly planted saplings around their feet, unfurl their fresh new leaves ready to begin the harvesting of another year's sun.

Below them, eager to catch the light before the leafy

They used to be known as azaleas, now they are all classified as rhododendrons but whatever the name this one still brings a magnificent blaze of lilac to the Lily Garden

canopy closes over, thousands of early wild flowers – bluebells, wood anemone, wild garlic, celandine, primrose – sparkle on the woodland floor, still with its covering of autumn gold.

And of course in mid-March, when Spring begins and the house, once again spic-and-span and the formal gardens reopen, it is time for the staff and volunteers who keep Mount Stewart running to gear up for another hectic season of visitors, events and entertainment.

As if trying to imitate the snow of winter this
frothing magnolia covers the ground with white

Loveliest of trees, the cherry now
Is hung with bloom along the bough

A E Housman

The magnificent rhododendrons, among the
oldest in the garden, tower over the driveway

**Joy in looking and comprehending
is nature's most beautiful gift**

Albert Einstein

Bushes flame against the dark woodland

Spring's first surge brings a pale green
flush to the tall beech trees

April hath put a spirit of youth in everything

William Shakespeare

Bluebells line the woodland track

Young saplings burst into a froth
of bright spring green between the
dark trunks of their elders

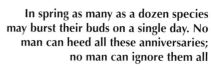

In spring as many as a dozen species
may burst their buds on a single day. No
man can heed all these anniversaries;
no man can ignore them all

Aldo Leopold

Now is the time of the illuminated woods
– when every leaf glows like a tiny lamp

J Burroughs

Just at the start of its long life, a young Magnolia is literally bursting to show what it can do

That God once loved a garden we learn in Holy writ,
And seeing gardens in the spring I can well credit it

Winifred Letts

Cherries and rhododendron seem to be trying to outdo each other in celebrating Spring

Spring shows what God can do with a drab and dirty world

Virgil Kraft

Mount Stewart's glorious array of rhododendron blooms epitomise the colourful joy and hope of Spring.

Giant Chinese rhododendrons create a high
wall of colour along the path known as Jubilee
Avenue, above the north side of the Lake

This tall rhododendron was blown to
the ground many years ago but still
puts on a fine show every Spring

Venus and Eurydice wait to welcome the first visitors of a new season to the grand entrance hall of a spring-cleaned and spic and span house, which opens in March each year. During the seven months they are open tens of thousands of people will be shown round the stately rooms of the house in guided tours. Opening day also features a Second Hand Book Fair, one of two each year, in which books donated by National Trust members and others raise thousand of pounds towards the upkeep of the house and garden.

A colourful lake view

Now every field is clothed with grass, and every tree with leaves; now
the woods put forth their blossoms and the year assumes its gay attire

Virgil

Spring on Rhododendron Hill

Swards of daffodils bring the spirit of
spring to the sweeping lawns

Down among the grass smaller beauties shine

Self-seeded primula bring colour
to the woodland edges

Wisteria brings early colour to the formal gardens

May – and a Cockchafer beetle sets out
in search of a place to lay its eggs – they
produce larvae which then spend up to
three years feeding on plant roots!

Primula, lilies and azaleas edge the lake in a burst of colours

Science has never drummed up quite as effective tranquilising agent as a sunny spring day

W Earl Hall

The annual Craft Fair is one of the 'big' events staged at Mount Stewart from Spring to Autumn. It allows some of Northern Ireland's most skilled crafts workers to showcase their talents and draws as many as 10,000 visitors.

Some turn up a bit early for the Craft Fair in May!

With a new state-of-the-art nursery and plant propagation unit now up and running, the Mount Stewart garden team can ensure a good supply of flowering plants and shrubs for their garden displays – and for sale in the garden shop, as well as supplying other National Trust properties

Lofty view of Mount Stewart's lake with early pale Spring colour beginning to spread round the shore

Lakeside
Beauty

Its garden artistry will fill you with wonder, its glorious rhododendrons in bloom with amazement but its lake, cradled in a landscape of ever-changing living colour, can bring pure delight all through the year.

If the gardens are the soul of Mount Stewart – the lake is its heart.

A grand house demands a grand parkland setting and Mount Stewart was given one 160 years ago when the third Lord Londonderry hired an army of labourers to excavate a lake on the site of what had been a gravel pit, the excavated material being used to build an earth dam and landscape the area around it. His original one was later enlarged but it was not until the time of Edith, Lady Londonderry that her creative planting ideas made it what it is.

Embraced by gentle drumlin slopes and encircled by an amazing diversity of plant life, trees stately and feathery, flowering shrubs from around the world and flowers that set the water's edge ablaze in spring, it is little wonder that thousands come every year just to enjoy the colourful walk around it or sit and take in the views – especially of the colourful foliage reflected in the water. They get two for the price of one!

The island of rushes and lilies is artificial, created to provide a refuge with privacy for wildlife

Sometimes quietly reflective, sometimes wind-rippled and sparkling, sometimes shrouded in drifting mist and sometimes even frozen over and white with snow, the five-acre lake is a constant while the land around it endlessly changes with the seasons.

And then there are its birds.

Mount Stewart may no longer be able to offer the sight of 10 pink flamingos picking their way through the

When I go into the countryside and see the sun and the green and everything flowering I say to myself Yes indeed, all that belongs to me!

Henri Rousseau

shallows, which it did for 17 years (they were a gift from King Fuad of Egypt in 1934), but its stately swans, chattering duck (always on the look-out for a tasty hand-out from visitors) and its other resident water-fowl, as well as visiting flocks of sea-birds, add yet another dimension – one which many, especially the young, enjoy as much as the flora.

Roll on spring…!

Winter 'lock-out' for these visiting seabirds

There's always an enthusiastic welcome for visitors with a bag of goodies

Serenity

Peaceful co-existence!

Nothing like a good stretch…!

Rising from the tranquil lake waters for more than 100 years this Japanese Pagoda was bought by Lord and Lady Londonderry during a visit to the Far East in 1904

Nature does not hurry, yet everything is accomplished

Lao Tzu

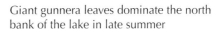

Giant gunnera leaves dominate the north bank of the lake in late summer

The richness of summer almost hides the towers
of Ti na nOg peeping coyly from the hillside

**Blessed be the Lord for the beauty of
summer and spring, for the air, the water,
the verdure and the song of birds**

Carl von Linnaeus

The lake is fed by a stream draining the high ground
to the north. These pictures show it in winter,
flowing in spate through the bare empty ground
and the same scene, transformed, in summer

Colour, colour – just everywhere!

Rest is not idleness, and to lie sometimes on the grass on a summer day listening to the murmer of water or watching the clouds float across the sky is hardly a waste of time

John Lubbock

Autumn and fallen leaves pattern the lake water

Waiting to take the plunge

Mount Stewart's swans are an iconic feature of the lake scene and most years they raise a family. This sequence of pictures shows the young ones developing from spring to late summer. Here the expectant father pulls out reed leaves to start building the family's nest near the shore

The proud parents keep a close watch on their tiny new chicks

Enough for one day – the young are herded back to the safety of the nest

By July they are growing rapidly

August – crossing the lake in stately convoy

September – The world calls –
time to stretch the wings!

93

Summer sees the full ordered luxuriance of the Italian Garden

Summer
in Full Colour

There is always colour to enjoy in the formal gardens around Mount Stewart house such as the bulbs or specimen rhododendron that open the season, but it is in high summer that they reach their full luxuriance with the beds overflowing with an eclectic diversity of the common and the exotic.

High summer is also the time of frenetic gardening activity too, with the cutting of the grass and trimming of the border hedges needed to keep the gardens immaculate – always a race to keep up with the growth! And of course the weeds are always pursuing their never-ending take-over bid for the well-fed soil.

Out in the woodland areas the leafy canopy has closed over but grasses and ferns have come into their own and where gaps in the cover allow light to shaft through there are new flowers to catch the eye – clumps of stately foxgloves, willowherbs, purple thistles…

In the semi-formal gardens the grassed areas will get their first cutting of the year in late summer, having been left to grow as wild-flower meadows, sparkling with buttercups, daisies and orchids.

Maples flame by the lakeside

On the great lawns the marquees go up for fairs and shows and weddings. Music, from classics to jazz, fills the air with Sunday afternoon and evening performances and there are guided walks around the gardens for those who want to know more. In the house the guides there, with their encyclopaedic knowledge of its history, are kept at full stretch showing visitors around.

And of course for people clearing their attics or looking for a bargain Saturday morning, car boot sales have become something of an institution!

Clumps of lilies flame in the formal gardens

Low sunlight strikes through the golden
umbrella of a weeping maple, silhouetting
the complexity of its branches

Many of the formerly close-cropped grass area are now allowed to grow into mid-summer as wild-flower meadows, but around the end of August, the flowering season done and flower seeds scattered, the swards are cut and taken away for composting

Waste not, want not – in an economy-minded piece of recycling an ancient iron gate, still with a stern keep-out warning notice, is pressed into use to keep branches etc from blocking a drainage pipe.

Keeping the high yew hedges that enclose the
Shamrock Garden in trim takes several weeks work
each summer, with much of the work, especially
the series of topiary figures that surmount them,
having to be done delicately with hand clippers.

A world-wide range of plants ensures a
long season of colour to be enjoyed in the
Lily Garden, seen here in late August

Among the most popular summer events at
Mount Stewart are the monthly Music on Sunday
and Jazz Sunday afternoons with music lovers
flocking to listen and maybe picnic with their
families and enjoy the 'music among the trees'

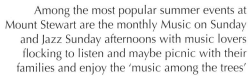

**A tree is more than first a seed, then
a stem, then a living trunk, then dead
timber. The tree is a slow enduring
force straining to win the sky**

Antoine de Saint-Exupery

All through the season (and in all weathers!), under the guidance of Mount Stewart's skilled professional gardeners, teams of volunteers work to maintain the flower beds and shrubberies to their international standards of excellence. Late autumn to early spring is the busiest time for other volunteer teams who work in the woodland areas trimming, felling, clearing 'weed' shrubs and planting new young trees. Altogether almost 50 volunteers give their time to maintaining the gardens and woodlands

**Gardening imparts an organic
perspective on the passage of time**

William Cowper

Summer afternoon – summer afternoon; to me those have always been the two most beautiful words in the English language

Henry James

Mount Stewart's Vehicles of Yesterday extravaganza, held annually on Fathers' Day, is one of its most popular attractions drawing thousands to view almost 120 classical and vintage cars and enjoy a great day out.

As well as their other skills the staff and volunteers
and Mount Stewart need to demonstrate considerable
traffic management expertise to avoid chaos
when thousands of cars arrive for big events!

The Reception area at Mount Stewart
– a very busy place, especially when
big events are being staged.

The terrace round the Sunk Garden

Everybody needs beauty as well as bread, places to stay in and pray in, where nature may heal and give strength to body and soul

John Muir

Come – explore and enjoy, the
Lily Wood seems to call

Earth laughs in flowers

Ralph Waldo Emerson

Orchids and buttercups celebrate summer together

A water lily smiles at the sun in one of
the Italian Garden's fountains

Everywhere throughout the woodlands clumps
of foxgloves spring up to welcome visitors

A demonstration of a more traditional method of extracting felled trees

It is the month of June
The month of leaves and roses
When pleasant sights salute the eyes
And pleasant scents the noses

N P Willis

The Lily Wood's exotic residents can give it a tropical look in summer.

With its elegance, gardens and woodlands Mount Stewart is now established as a place to have the big day. Wedding ceremonies can be held in the mansion and post-wedding celebrations in marquees on the lawns or in the Temple of the Winds

A sudden wind brings down a high branch
across one of the paths – clearing it becomes
a priority that day for garden staff

**There is always music among the
trees in the garden, but our hearts
must be very quiet to hear it**

Minnie Aumonier

By July the woodlands are dense as young trees
in full leaf spread their growing branches

The terrace walls of the Sunk Garden drape themselves in purple for the spring

Gardens
to Delight

If asked to sum up the essential spirit and charm of Mount Stewart's gardens in just two words, none would be more fitting than 'whimsical exuberance'.

Although at just 80 acres modest in area compared with some of its other famous gardens, it ranks among Europe's greatest and none other can boast such a wealth of diverse garden experiences in such a modest space.

Almost a century ago Almost a century ago the wife of the new master of the estate the Seventh Marquess, took a traditional stately home landscape of grass and trees around the house and led the way in developing a totally new 'pleasure garden' concept, in effect extending the living area of the house with a series of formal outdoor 'rooms' filled with colour and a mixture of classical and whimsical design – the Italian Garden, the Spanish, the Mairi, the Sunk, the Shamrock – each distinctive, each delightful.

Moving away from the garden rooms the formality, with its parterres, pergolas and terraces, pavilions, eccentric statues and Italian flavour, gives way gradually to semi-formal flowering shrub areas – the Lily Wood,

Sitting patiently for almost a century this faithful pet now wears a coat of colourful algae. Along the wall beneath this fellow are plaques in memory of a number of dogs – pets of family members over the years.

Rhododendron Hill – where rhododendrons (her passion), magnolias, cherries and other exotics blaze with colour, to water gardens around the lake, and eventually 'wild' woodland with stately trees and drifts of wild flowers.

Money was no object and she was able to scour the nurseries of the world for plants (one single order to

Reflected in the waters of the fountain, the gold leaves of the Vine Gate lead from the Italian Garden into the less formal Lily Wood.

an English nursery was for 17,000 tulip and narcissi bulbs!) to indulge her passion for growing the rare, exotic and tender, which flourished in the semi-tropical micro-climate, and which resulted in a staggering diversity of botanical treasures.

The war years were a set-back but this adventurous approach has been revived since 1970 with the National Trust's ongoing restoration programme for the gardens, which was led for 30 years until his retirement in 2000, by the outstanding Head Gardener, Nigel Marshall.

Writing of her guiding principal in a booklet she wrote for the National Trust after passing the gardens into its care, their creator wrote: *'Gardens are meant to be lived in and enjoyed'*. She could equally have said 'Gardens are meant to be fun' – and Mount Stewart's are all of that!

The famous Red Hand of Ulster in the Shamrock Garden. It is a right hand (assuming it is palm down). It was originally a left hand, that of the McDonnell clan, but this later came to be not very politically correct for a leading Unionist family so it was changed.

The planting of the Red Hand is changed through the spring and summer to ensure continuity of colour. These spring tulips are the first to blaze

The Red Hand stands out brightly in this aerial picture of the Shamrock Garden

A young family relax under one of Mount Stewart's venerable giants, a Monterey Cypress

Stone planters against the dark ewe hedging provide provide bright splashes under the pergola around the Sunk Garden

Early spring and the gardens begin to fill with colour

**'Tis my faith that every flower
Enjoys the air it breathes!**

William Wordsworth

The Sunk Garden's beds blaze with colour in spring –
later the colour scheme turns to blue as delphiniums
and other summer plants take their place

The rustic sandstone Sundial Steps link
the Sunk Garden and the Lily Wood

**When you have only two pennies left
in the world – buy a loaf of bread
with one and a lily with the other**

Chinese proverb

The blue and white planting scheme of the secluded Mairi Garden surrounds the fountain with its statue of the young Lady Mairi

A hoverfly enjoys one of the rose blooms in the Mairi Garden

**What is life if, full of care,
We have no time to stop and stare**

W H Davis

Agapanthus line the paved path to Tir na nOg

The Wounded Stag (with arrow sticking from
its back) – one of the Shamrock Garden's
topiary hunting scene fantasies

The carved stone horoscope table in
the Spanish Garden summerhouse

As a work of art a great garden is not simply a collection
of plants ... it expresses human values and spiritual ideals

John Sales

Raised beds overflow with colour in high summer

The elegant Swan Gates are opened in March
each year to welcome visitors to enjoy the formal
gardens for another spring and summer

Two dodos flank the east entrance to the
Italian garden- between them the Ark from
which the mythical animals have emerged

Almost more at risk from winter frosts than the
plants in the Italian Garden are the 90 year old
sculptures of fantasy animals which are such a
treasured feature. To save them from the risk of
damage from rain and cold they spend the winter
snuggled up in waterproof and windproof fabric.

Frolicsome fun in a formal garden? Pretty rare but uniquely abundant at Mount Stewart with its parade of whimsical animal sculptures around the walls of the Italian Garden. The sculptures represent members of the 'Ark Club' an invitation-only group of Edith, Lady Londonderry's aristocratic friends, who were given animal pseudonyms by her and who got together regularly at her London home during and after the First World War for a bit of craic. Edith presided over the Club and had caricature sculptures made for her garden. (The sculptures were made by local craftsman Thomas Beattie and were a pioneering use of cast concrete for such work. He also made the coping stones for all the sandstone walls)

Around the garden are several sculpted panels depicting a fox and a phoenix

Sculpture is the art of the intelligence

Pablo Picasso

May – and the beds fill with colour

King of all he surveys

A mythical creature from the deep keeps an eye
on visitors from his dark lair below the ark

A bright fern flourishes in its classical home

Rhododendrons rain colour on the garden walls

Like sentinals standing along the south side of the Italian Garden are a line of tall pillars, topped with flower pots held aloft by rather smug looking orang-utans with cloven feet sitting on the shoulders of somewhat bewildered looking humans. Their meaning has not been explained – but they certainly have a Darwinian feel about them!

Each flower is a soul blossoming out to nature

Gerard de Nerval

Some in bloom, others ready to burst out, this
clump of poppies makes a delightful composition

**If you have never been thrilled
to the very edges of your soul by
a flower in spring bloom, maybe
your soul has never been in bloom**

Terri Guillemets

These azaleas have been producing their blaze
of orange in the Sunk Garden since 1923

Stately delphiniums strut their
stuff every summer

This massive weather-sculpted tree trunk
greets visitors just inside the entrance gate

An oasis of tranquility in the Lily Wood

Wisteria Tunnel

Opposite the entrance to the reception area a beautifully rustic high fence of woven willow stems has attracted the admiration of many visitors. However it is not there just for ornament – it will be there for about four years to protect from winter's north winds the tender rhododendrons and other shrubs that have been planted behind it as part of the major restoration of the Mairi Garden and what was known as the Fountain Walk. The delightful Wisteria Tunnel has been extended and in a few years a long-disappeared row of high evergreen arches will once more line the walk. This work was the first carried out (in 2010 and 2011) of a number of major renovation and restoration projects planned over a six-year period.

The Wisteria tunnel has been more than doubled in length

Tender new shrubs shelter behind the willow fencing

133

A volunteer enjoys a peaceful afternoon tending the plants

The Silent Army

Nature struts her stuff like nowhere else, the big house opens its windows on a fascinating past and the National Trust's expertise ensures it will remain to be enjoyed – but the lifeblood of the Mount Stewart experience is its 'silent army' – the teams of volunteers without whom it just could not exist.

Although naturally not all are ever available at any one time the gardens have almost 200 volunteers offering their time and skills and filling a range of roles in every aspect of the work of running it – some doing a day, or maybe more, a week, others a few hours whenever they can manage it. Together they contribute well over 15,000 hours a year!

Mount Stewart has just under 30 permanent staff, augmented during the busy summer by more than 40 seasonal employees, but with 80 acres of gardens and woodlands, a reception desk, a big house to show visitors around, a shop, a restaurant, education and visitor services, flowers to be arranged, a plant propagation and sales unit, a lot of admin… all helping hands are welcome!

The smooth running of the big crowd-pulling annual events such as the Craft Fair is also due in a big way to the contribution – from guiding visitors to managing the traffic – of volunteers.

Volunteers tidy the beds in the Spanish Garden.

More than a quarter of the volunteers work in the garden, work that can range from helping with tree or rhododendron clearance to dead-heading flowers in the formal displays – a very pleasant way to pass a warm summer day.

In a recent initiative that has really taken off and making a fast growing contribution to maintaining and developing the gardens is 'corporate volunteering' with the Trust inviting organisations to let groups of employees get away from their desks for a day to join together in doing something totally different.

The contribution volunteers make to Mount Stewart is incalculable – but the volunteers would all say that the enjoyment and satisfaction it brings them is more than reward enough – sure the craic's great!.

It's two for the price of one when the trees' glorious autumn colours are repeated in their reflections in the lake

Autumn
— The Grand Finale

Evening sun makes the autumn trees flame with colour

Summer fades as the sun sinks lower in the sky, another glorious performance finished, the gardens pack away their colourful costumes, the entertainers have gone, the House closed down; it is as if the stage has been cleared for the grand finale of the Mount Stewart year – autumn.

The countless millions of leaves that formed the high woodland canopy and danced in the lakeside breezes have done their summer's job too – converting sunlight into food for the trees and shrubs. As days shorten and temperatures fall growth stops, the chlorophyll that greens the leaves breaks up leaving them in their glowing shades of yellow, red, orange, purple – dressed and ready to cascade down in the greatest show of the year.

Not all trees can contribute to the autumn colour show; ash and sycamore don't have what it takes – even oak isn't great. Fortunately Mount Stewart has more than enough of the best performers – mighty beech, chestnut, lime, and the daintier birch and many different varieties of native and Japanese maple which around the lakeside especially put on some of the brightest colour performances of the year.

With some trees, such as lime, the leaves drop one by one as they 'die' and its fall is spread over a month or more. Others like to wear their autumn capes as long as they can until a sudden frost or a gale brings them down all at once in a cascade that lays the gold carpet that makes the woodlands magic places to walk through.

The lakeside loses nothing in terms
of colour when autumn comes

Autumn colours on the go

A venerable giant spreads a golden carpet around his feet

**Everyone must take time to sit
and watch the leaves turn**

Elizabeth Lawrence

Giant rhododendron leaves hang on as long as they can

Time for quiet reflection

By all these lovely tokens
September days are here
With summer's best of weather
And autumn's best of cheer

Anon

Winter is an etching, spring a watercolour, summer an oil painting and autumn a mosaic of them all

Stanley Horowitz

Shades of the turning year

**Autumn is a second spring
when every leaf is a flower**

Albert Camus

I walked along the edge of the lake and was treated to the crunch and rustle of leaves with every step I made. The acoustics of this season are different and all sounds, no matter how hushed, are as crisp as autumn air

Eric Sloane

A splash of gold among the green shrubberies of Rhododendron Hill

Autumn carpets the stairs to Tir na nOg

**A tangerine and russet cascade
Of kaleidoscopic leaves
Creates a tapestry of autumn magic
Upon the emerald carpet
of fading summer**

Judith Lindberg

The topiary harp in the Shamrock Garden gets a new backdrop

Colours flare in the Lily Wood

A track-walk beckons

A long-abandoned relic of farming days
blends with the autumn shades

Youthful trees put on a cheerful
display to end the season

**Autumn is more than three months bounded
by an equinox and a solstice – it is a summing
up without the finality of year's end**

Hal Borland

**A woodland in full colour is awesome
as a forest fire, in magnitude at least,
but a single tree is like a dancing
tongue of flame to warm the heart**

Hal Borland

Mount Stewart's woodlands and
shrubberies are a paradise for fungi
fanatics in autumn. This fly agaric brings
a bright if brief splash of colour.

As if Mount Stewart doesn't put on a colourful enough show for autumn, the annual Hallowe'en Enchanted Evening event takes it to dramatic levels, with the floodlighting of trees and shrubberies , bonfires and of course ghosties and ghoulies aplenty. The reflection of the floodlit autumn trees in the lake waters is a breathtaking spectacle.

This is the autumn-coloured group of trees seen on p149 – now floodlit for Hallowe'en.

Harvest time each year is celebrated at Mount Stewart with its two-day 'Food Glorious Food' event where visitors can indulge themselves in a wide range of gastronomic delights – and show off their skills.

JOINT WINNER PRETTIEST CUPCAKE

Among the items on display at the Food Fair a collection of Victorian kitchen ware from the 'big house'. The big container in the centre was the measure of a 'bushel' of vegetables or fruit or corn.

The family, still resident in the house, lent some of the china they continue to use for a display given by the National Trust in the Central Hall. Some of this china was used during the 1903 Royal visit when King Edward and Queen Alexandra stayed at Mount Stewart – one of many visits by members of Europe's royalty and political elite.

The big clean-up

The close-down of the big house at the end of October marks the start of months of hard work – the cleaning of every object on display and every item of furniture, from the chandeliers to cushions to paintings and carpets. Moveable objects are packed away in storage waiting to be cleaned during the winter, display cabinets are emptied and cleaned along with their contents and the rooms 'put to bed' under dust sheets. Most of the delicate work is done by staff and volunteers – some are pictured here starting the dusting using just very soft hair brushes – but many items have to be handled by specialists. Finally everything, once again pristine and sparkling, is put back for display ready for the opening of another season in March.

The crystal chandeliers get the soft-brush treatment to remove dust before their winter rest.

Every item of furniture is cleaned and inspected for damage before being tucked away under its dust-sheet for the five months until being put on view again in March each year.

Safe and cosy - the public rooms are put
to bed and tucked in for the winter.

Newtownards Lodge, the original main entrance to the estate

The Story
of a Great Garden

It is quite likely that some of the beeches that today seem to scrape the skies, or the gnarled oaks that wear skirts of bluebells before their deep shade darkens the ground, might have already been rooted in the soil of a small estate on the shores of Strangford Lough when Alexander Stewart came to view it more than 250 years ago.

Stewart was a wealthy businessman of Scottish planter stock who lived in North Donegal. In 1737 he married wealthy heiress Mary Cowan and the advice of the trustees of his wife's dowry was to invest it in land and property, ideally in the more prosperous east side of Ireland – then, as now, 'location location, location' was everything.

In 1744 he paid a bit over £42,000 for what had been identified as a good investment: the manors of Newtownards and Comber – and the smaller estate, Temple Crone, a few miles to the south. He established his family home in Newtownards and on the other estate built a small weekend 'cabin', plus other ones for guests, and called it Mount Pleasant.

His family and his businesses flourished and within four generations – and a few more lucrative marriages – had become among the most influential and wealthy of Britain's social and political elite, some of them major players on the international stage. Meanwhile the estate's landscape continued to evolve too, the trees growing accompanied now by hundreds of new ones planted as woodlands and shelter belts to deflect the south-westerly winds blowing across the Lough (without which today's more refined gardens could not exist!). Gradually the estate evolved into graceful parkland surrounding a grand mansion. The stage was being set but it would be more than 150 years before it blossomed into an internationally acclaimed botanical treasure-house.

Alexander continued to enjoy his weekend retreat until his death in 1781 when the property was inherited by his elder son Robert. An ambitious man who rose rapidly through the ranks of the peerage – baron, viscount, earl and eventually in 1816 the 1st Marquess of Londonderry – he had great fondness for the estate, lived there much of the time and raised 11 children. He renamed it Mount Stewart and in the 1780s built a new wing and engaged landscape designers to improve the parkland around it.

At the same time, in tune with the prevailing fashion, he commissioned the building of one of Mount Stewart's best loved and iconic features, the Temple of the Winds, with its hilltop views over Strangford Lough

Although owned and maintained by the National Trust, Tir na nOg (the land of the ever-young of Celtic mythology) on its high hillside overlooking the lake is the private Londonderry family burying ground. The carved stone sarcophagi of the Seventh Marquess and his wife Lady Londonderry lie on either side of the carriage entrance arch. Although not generally open to visitors it can be viewed through the wrought-iron gates at each side and its views over the gardens can be seen from the top of the steps to the right of the tower.

Two round 'temples' form the front corners of Tir na nOg. This is the door of one, thick bog oak planks held together with ornate and massive iron hinges across County Down to the Mourne Mountains and its exquisite interior, which is modelled on a romantic hilltop building in Athens.

He also built the must-have for self-sufficient estates – a 10-acre walled garden with extensive greenhouses, for the growing of flowers, vegetables and fruit. Almost a mile from the house it is not part of the National Trust property, but is the location of its newly created propagation unit, raising plants for the garden displays, for sale to the public and to supply other Trust properties.

Robert had had even bigger plans for his demesne by the sea but the cost of furthering the family's political ambitions for his son, also Robert, strained even his finances. A brilliant politician Robert Junior became Lord Castlereagh in own right before succeeding to the Londonderry title as 2nd Marquess in 1821 and was one of the leading European political and diplomatic figures of this turbulent time. (The set of chairs in the Dining Room of the House are those used by the delegates at the Congress of Vienna after the Napoleonic Wars at which he was a principal organiser).

Although he grew up in and loved Mount Stewart the demands of his career kept him away most of his adult life and his influence on the development of the estate was limited. In the end, broken by the pressures of his life, he committed suicide in 1822, only a year after succeeding to the title.

And for Mount Stewart things were about to change!

Robert was succeeded by his half-brother Charles, a flamboyant and dashing career soldier with a record of bravery and leadership (and a dedicated visitor to bedrooms not his own!).

The family was already wealthy but when in 1819, seven years after the death of his first wife, Charles married a woman who was reputedly the wealthiest heiress in England, Frances Anne Vane-Tempest, who came not just with a virtually limitless fortune but two large estates and a very profitable coal-mining operation in Co Durham. Through her mother, the Countess of Antrim, she also owned large swathes of land on Ireland's north coast.

The couple did not stint themselves either in the ostentation of their lifestyle at the pinnacle of British society or in creating even grander houses to enjoy it in and to accommodate their ever-growing collection of art and antiquities, and Mount Stewart was one of their most favoured homes. Between 1845 and 1850 the existing house was trebled in size and the original building now forms just the west wing of the present impressive mansion (the 'junction' between the two, to the right of the giant entrance portico, is marked by a distinct difference in the pattern of the masonry). Built to impress, it does that in style as the huge number of visitors today testify.

A grand mansion with a grand social life swirling around it demands a grand parkland and what the huge extension was to the house, the inspired creation of a lake big enough to fish in was to the gardens – totally transforming a fairly neglected sweep of sloping grassland disfigured by a gravel pit.

Later the culverting of the stream that drains the lake down to the sea also allowed the laying out of the level lawns that are the setting for so many activities

Edith, Lady Londonderry's sitting room, one of the ornately furnished 'windows' on a bygone age that visitors can see in a tour of the House

today. Many of the stateliest trees and the now majestic rhododendrons that bring so much colour today were planted at this time.

Charles's flamboyant life ended in 1854 and his devoted wife raised a number of monuments to him. Most dramatic is the great tower on Scrabo Hill – which is still Londonderry land, now leased by the Government as a Country Park. It used to be a common belief that the Tower was paid for by grateful tenants for his charity to them during the Potato Famine, which hit the area hard just at the time he was starting to splash out on Mount Stewart, but in fact he had done precious little for them and the money was raised among his political and social friends in the establishment. It must be acknowledged however that, even if not motivated by thoughts of 'famine relief', the work on the house

and the lake must have created welcome employment in the area.

The next two holders of the Londonderry title both chose, except for occasional visits, to live at the homes of their wives – the 4th Marquess at Powerscourt in Co Wicklow and the 5th in Wales with the result that Mount Stewart was reduced largely to a care and maintenance status for virtually the rest of the century. The gardens were typical of the time, mostly sweeping lawns with herbaceous borders and dotted with trees and shrubberies of flowering shrubs such as rhododendron and magnolia.

Although they only actually stayed there a few times a year, things were improved considerably by the 6th Marquess (he inherited in 1884) and his wife Theresa who took a renewed interest in encouraging the enhancement of the gardens and wrote glowingly of them. (The giant eucalyptus trees that are such magnificent sentinels around today's formal gardens were grown from seed by Theresa, but the oldest of them was actually raised by the wife of the 3rd Marquess). Theresa liked to refer to Mount Stewart as 'my villa by the sea' High spot of their time there was a visit in 1903 by King Edward and Queen Alexandra, with whom Theresa was very friendly. This would certainly have acted as a spur to smartening up house and gardens. (The two copper beech flanking the entrance to the North Lawns were planted by the King and Queen).

Although Mount Stewart was an important item in the family's extensive property portfolio (the entire estate is just under 1,000 acres, all prosperous farmland except

Packed with history – another of the
rooms that visitors can enjoy

The grand drawing room – scene
of many stately gatherings

Edith, Lady Londonderry, the woman whose passion and stylish creativity created what is acclaimed as one of Europe's great gardens. This portrait, which can be seen in the House, shows her in the uniform of the Women's Legion which she founded during the First World War

for the 97 acres now owned by the National Trust) it is likely that as a residence it would have become more and more marginalised in the affairs of the family – and certainly its service as a military hospital during the First World War would not have helped – had not Edith, Lady Londonderry, wife of Charles, the 7th Marquess, who inherited in 1915, appeared on the stage with her enthusiastic genius for taking garden design to a new level. She also modernised and transformed the house into a home of elegant luxury and warmth whose hospitality became renowned.

Having visited Mount Stewart before 1915, she was initially less than impressed, describing it as 'the darkest and saddest place' she had ever stayed in, with overgrown trees shutting out the light from the house. She grew to appreciate its potential charms however and by the time her husband succeeded to the title she was asking him why they would ever want to live anywhere else!

The demands of her position at the heart of London society meant she had to supervise the creation of her garden dream from afar much of the time. With the help of advice from the owners of some of Northern Ireland's other inspired gardens and the talents of Thomas Bolas, the outstanding head gardener who 'came with the estate' in 1915, she drew up her plans and immediately after the war, with the help of labour provided by 20 demobilised servicemen in addition to the garden staff she began the work of sculpting the landscape, felling trees and excavating the sloping ground below the house to create the level terraces where her captivating garden 'rooms' would take shape and flourish in their unique 'sub-tropical' micro-climate.

She was not a novice garden designer, having created two at other family houses, but Mount Stewart allowed her the opportunity to pursue her exuberant and flamboyant tastes and love of the exotic and rare. The opportunity to give Mount Stewart her undivided attention came when her husband became Minister for Education in the newly formed Government of Northern Ireland in 1921 and the family made it their home.

She devoted the next 20 years to creating a garden – or rather a complex of gardens with many different and contrasting facets – that was not only among the most beautiful and artistic in the British Isles, if not Europe, but unique – because of its sheltered micro-climate that she knew how to exploit to the full – in its displays of plants that would normally only be seen growing under glass or in warmer climes and for which she had a passion.

She acquired plants and seed from collectors around the world and often sponsored expeditions to remote areas, especially the southern hemisphere and the Far East. Her great passion was rhododendrons, sometimes planting them in groups of 30 or 50 and the display their successors (regarded by some as the most important collection in the British Isles) put on every spring are still arguably the garden's greatest glory, starting in February and lasting well into summer.

During the late 20s and the 30s the gardens were opened to the public two days a week and major events were staged in aid of a number of charities.

The restrictions of the Second World War, shortage of staff and difficulty in obtaining new plant material hit the gardens badly and after the war and until his death in 1949 her priority became the nursing of her ill husband. However her determination prevailed. She employed extra gardeners (not easy to find), replanted abandoned beds and gradually got her creations back their former glory. She continued working in the gardens herself and providing plants for them (collectors round the world continued to send her new discoveries) – even after she, her daughter and son-in-law donated them to the National Trust in 1955 – and up to her death in 1959.

With her death total management of the gardens fell to the National Trust, its head gardeners and advisors – with the support and encouragement of her daughter Lady Mairi, who continued to live at Mount Stewart until her death 50 years later, in 2009.

Today Lady Mairi's daughter, Lady Rose Lauritzen, continues the family's dedication to supporting the National Trust in ensuring that the spirit of her grandmother's achievement in creating one of the great gardens of Europe can be enjoyed by generations to come.

Cottage
Publications

For more information and to see our other titles, please visit our website
www.cottage-publications.com
or alternatively you can contact us as follows:–

Telephone: +44 (0)28 9188 8033
Fax: +44 (0)28 9188 8063

Cottage Publications
is an imprint of
Laurel Cottage Ltd.,
15 Ballyhay Road,
Donaghadee, Co. Down,
N. Ireland, BT21 0NG